Workbook 3

Caribbean Primary Social Studies
Our Caribbean Community

LISA GREENSTEIN

HODDER EDUCATION
AN HACHETTE UK COMPANY

Acknowledgements

The Publishers would like to thank the following for permission to reproduce copyright material.

Photo acknowledgements

p. 4 © Vilna Robotav 3d/Adobe Stock Photo; **p. 24** © Solarysys/Alamy Stock Photo; **p. 63** © Verizon Media Brand

Every effort has been made to trace all copyright holders, but if any have been inadvertently overlooked, the Publishers will be pleased to make the necessary arrangements at the first opportunity.

Although every effort has been made to ensure that website addresses are correct at time of going to press, Hodder Education cannot be held responsible for the content of any website mentioned in this book. It is sometimes possible to find a relocated web page by typing in the address of the home page for a website in the URL window of your browser.

Hachette UK's policy is to use papers that are natural, renewable and recyclable products and made from wood grown in well-managed forests and other controlled sources. The logging and manufacturing processes are expected to conform to the environmental regulations of the country of origin.

Orders: please contact Hachette UK Distribution, Hely Hutchinson Centre, Milton Road, Didcot, Oxfordshire, OX11 7HH. Telephone: +44 (0)1235 827827. Email education@hachette.co.uk Lines are open from 9 a.m. to 5 p.m., Monday to Friday. You can also order through our website: ww.hoddereducation.com

ISBN: 9781510480742

© Lisa Greenstein 2021

First published in 2021 by

Hodder Education (a trading division of Hodder & Stoughton Limited),

An Hachette UK Company

Carmelite House

50 Victoria Embankment

London EC4Y 0DZ

www.hoddereducation.com

The authorised representative in the EEA is Hachette Ireland, 8 Castlecourt Centre, Dublin 15, D15 XTP3, Ireland (email: info@hbgi.ie)

Impression number   10 9 8 7 6 5 4 3 2

Year   2025

All rights reserved. Apart from any use permitted under UK copyright law, no part of this publication may be reproduced or transmitted in any form or by any means, electronic or mechanical, including photocopying and recording, or held within any information storage and retrieval system, without permission in writing from the publisher or under licence from the Copyright Licensing Agency Limited. Further details of such licences (for reprographic reproduction) may be obtained from the Copyright Licensing Agency Limited, www.cla.co.uk

Cover by Marc Monés from Davila Illustration Agency

Illustrations by Vian Oelofsen

Typeset in FS Albert 12/16 by IO Publishing CC

Printed by Ashford Colour Ltd

A catalogue record for this title is available from the British Library.

Contents

How to use this book — 4

Caribbean people
1. The Caribbean people: who are we? — 5
2. The arrival of our ancestors — 9
3. Why did our ancestors come to the Caribbean? — 11
4. How our ancestors created our Caribbean culture — 13

Locating the Caribbean
5. The Caribbean region — 15
6. Large and small countries — 17
7. Groups of countries — 20
8. How far? — 23

The Caribbean environment
9. Natural features — 24
10. Natural disasters — 28
11. Preparing for natural disasters — 33
12. The human environment — 36

Work and occupations
13. Why do people work? — 37
14. Jobs in different industries — 38
15. Resources and employment — 39
16. Major Caribbean industries — 43
17. Trade between Caribbean countries — 46

Caribbean nations
18. National leaders — 48
19. Belonging to a Caribbean nation — 50
20. People are national symbols — 55
21. National celebrations — 56

Caribbean cultural patterns
22. The way we live today — 58
23. Cultural links — 60
24. Sharing our culture using ICT — 61

How to use this book

Welcome to Caribbean Primary Social Studies Workbook 3. The activities here will help you learn as you work through Book 3, Our Caribbean Community. This workbook will start to prepare you for the Caribbean Primary Exit Assessment (CPEA) and other similar assessments. As you work through each chapter in the book, complete as many of the activities and exercises as you can. There may be some information that you do not know. This means you need to do some research. Research means working to find out information. You can do research in different ways:

- ✓ Visit a library, and find the information in books.
- ✓ Observe people, things and activities around you.
- ✓ Ask questions to members of your family and your community.
- ✓ Do internet searches, and find websites with more information.
- ✓ Think of places where the information might be available, for example a business, or a tourist information centre.

1 The Caribbean people: who are we?

Living together as one

1. Find two photographs of yourself – one from within the last 6 months, and one from when you were younger. Glue the two photographs here. Around the photographs, write the different ways that you have changed as you have grown older.

2. We live in webs of relationships. We have families and close friends, but we also have a wider community made up of extended family, acquaintances, teacher and other people we know. In this web, fill in the names of the people in your life. You may want to connect the bubbles with lines, or write more about each relationship around the bubbles.

Unit 1 The Caribbean people: who are we?

Living together as one

1 Read the information and answer the questions.

> Not all children live with their own parents. If both of a child's parents are unable to care for the child, care is provided by other people. Some children are **orphans**. This means they do not have parents to look after them. Some countries have **orphanages**, where orphans live together and receive care from people who are employed to look after them. Sometimes a family may **foster** (look after) a child who needs care. Usually a **foster family** is not related to the child, and the child may not stay permanently. If the child goes to live with relatives, such as aunts or uncles or grandparents, this is known as **kinship care**. If a child is legally **adopted**, that means the adults looking after him or her become the legal parents and the child becomes permanently part of that family. Each country has special systems that regulate foster care, orphanages and adoption. This is important to make sure that children are taken care of.

a What do we call an institution that employs people to look after children that do not have parents?

b Kim lives with her father's cousin and their family. What kind of care is this?

c What is the main difference between adoption and foster care?

d Explain why it is important for a country to provide services such as orphanages, foster care and adoption services.

e Find out about an organisation that looks after orphaned children in your country. Complete the fact file.

★ fact file

- ✪ Name of organisation: ....
- ✪ Address and contact details: ....
- ✪ More about what they do: ....

Caribbean people

Understanding abuse

Children have the right to live in a family, to feel loved, and to be safe from **abuse**. Child abuse is any treatment that endangers a child's mental, physical or emotional wellbeing. Types of abuse:

* **Physical** abuse harms a child's body and causes physical pain or injury.
* **Verbal** abuse includes harmful words, name-calling, threats, harsh criticism and undue blaming.
* **Sexual** abuse includes unwanted or inappropriate touching and forced sexual contact.
* **Psychological** abuse harms a child's emotional wellbeing. Threatening behaviour, lying, breaking promises and ignoring a child are examples of psychological abuse. The three types of abuse listed above overlap with psychological abuse too.

If a child is in an abusive family, they may need special protection, such as being moved to a foster family.

1. What should you do if someone you know is suffering from abuse at home? Discuss this with your group, and write your ideas below.

2. Find out a phone number or hotline that children can use if they need to report abuse. Write it here:

 :

7

Unit 1 The Caribbean people: who are we?

Discrimination and stereotyping

Discrimination takes place when people treat others unfairly, especially because of their age, gender, race or religion. One form of discrimination is **stereotyping**, where we characterise all people belonging to a particular group as being the same in some way.

1. Discuss each statement below in pairs. Explain:
   a who is being discriminated against
   b why the statement is wrong or unfair
   c what you would say or do in response.

   > You can't play basketball with us. You're too short.

   > You must be good at Maths because you look Asian.

   > This isn't a game for girls.

   > We don't want you in our group because you work so slowly in class.

2. Have you ever experienced discrimination? If you wish, write about your own experience here.

2 The arrival of our ancestors

Changing families

Families change as time goes on. People grow and get older. People get married. Some people move to other places. Birth and death change our families.

1. Draw a family tree showing the members of your family. If possible, show four generations.

HINT
'Four generations' means you, your parents, your grandparents and great-grandparents.

2. On your family tree, circle the names of family members that are no longer living.

3. If possible, identify any of your family members who arrived or settled in the Caribbean, or who emigrated or went to live somewhere else. Write their names, and where they came from or settled.

Unit 2 The arrival of our ancestors

Columbus' voyage

1. This map shows the route that Columbus took to the Caribbean on four different trips. Trace the first route in red, the second route in orange, the third route in green, and the fourth route in blue.

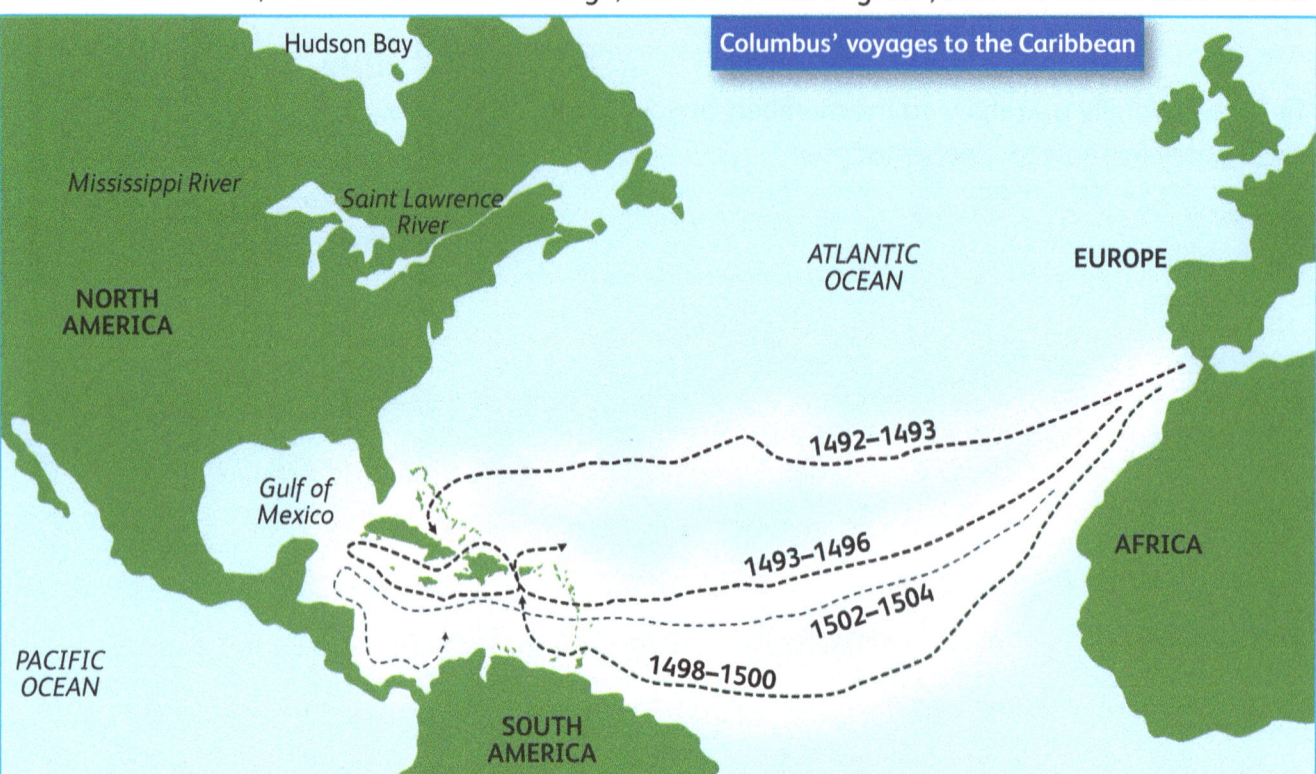

2. The islands of the Caribbean have been colonised by different European countries at different times. Use the internet to research islands claimed by each of these European colonisers. Fill in the islands, and the years they were ruled, in this table. Find each island on a map in your atlas.

Spain (Spanish)	France (French)	Netherlands (Dutch)	Britain (English)

# Why did our ancestors come to the Caribbean?

Describing historical events

> A historical **event** is something that happened in the past. Describing an event means telling about something that happened. To find out what happened, we use **sources** of information such as books, newspaper articles, documents from the past and accounts that other people have told us. It is important to understand that every source comes from someone's particular point of view.

1 Which group of people were living in the Caribbean long before the European settlers arrived?

_____

2 Do you agree that the Europeans discovered the Caribbean? Why or why not?

_____

_____

3 Describe the events that led the European settlers to start bringing enslaved people to the Caribbean.

_____

_____

_____

_____

4 a Which important event took place in the 1800s?

_____

b Which new groups of people arrived in the Caribbean as a result of this event?

_____

5 Historical events often involve acts of bravery, selflessness and determination. Discuss this in your class. Tell stories about historical figures (people) who have shown these qualities. If possible, write a few sentences about one of these people here.

_____

_____

_____

_____

Unit 3 Why did our ancestors come to the Caribbean?

Different groups

1 The Amerindian people have lived in the Caribbean for thousands of years. Most other groups have only arrived in the last 500 years. Read in your textbook about the different groups that started arriving in the 1400s, and write more about them.

Group of people	Main reasons for arrival, what they wanted to do here
Spanish	
British	
French	
Dutch	
West Africans	
East Indians	
Chinese	

2 How do you fit into the history of the Caribbean? Did anyone in your family come from these groups? How does it feel to learn this history? Write your thoughts here.

_____
_____
_____
_____
_____

4 How our ancestors created our Caribbean culture

Different groups brought aspects of our culture

Around the name of each group, write or draw some things that they brought, introduced or invented that is still a part of Caribbean culture today.

- Amerindians
- Europeans
- Indian
- Asian groups
- Chinese
- West Africans

13

Unit 4 How our ancestors created our Caribbean culture

Art of our community

People can express themselves and their culture through works of art, such as paintings, sculptures, crafts, murals and photography. If possible, visit a place, such as a museum or gallery, with works of art by people in your community. You may also find artworks in books or on websites. Choose one of the works of art. Write about it here, and draw a picture of it in the space provided.

Name of artwork: ....

Artist: ....

Medium: ....

Date: ....

Description: ....

....

....

Picture:

....

....

....

....

....

....

5 The Caribbean region

My country and neighbouring countries

1. My country is _____. The nearest neighbouring countries are:
   _____
   _____

2. The community I live in is called _____.
   Some of the neighbouring communities on the same island are:
   _____
   _____

3. Identify four important places in your country or in other Caribbean countries. Write the name of each place, and a few sentences about why it is important. If possible, draw or glue a picture too.

Unit 5 The Caribbean region

Important places in the Caribbean region

1. Trace or draw a map of a part of the Caribbean region you are interested in. Mark some important places on your map.

2. Write a sentence each about some of the important places on your map.

_____
_____
_____
_____

6 Large and small countries

Independent island countries

Today, most Caribbean countries are **independent** states, which are not ruled or governed by any foreign country. Before becoming independent, many countries first moved to becoming **associated states**. This meant that they controlled their own constitution and governments, but still kept an association with the former foreign ruling country, which took responsibility for foreign affairs and defence.

On this map, colour each independent (I) or associated (A) state a different colour, and label it with I or A.

17

Unit 6 Large and small countries

Passports and visas

A **passport** is an official booklet that you get from the government to prove your identity and citizenship. Whenever you enter or leave a country, you show your passport to prove that you have permission to be there. When you travel to other countries, you may need a **visa**. A visa is a form of permission to enter a country where you are not a citizen.

1. Look at a real passport or a picture of a passport. Draw a sketch of it here and show what you can see on the cover. It should include:
   - the country
   - the word PASSPORT
   - the national crest.

   Are there any other symbols or emblems on the passport? What do they mean?

2. Think of a country you would like to visit. Find out the visa requirements for visiting that country. Write about it here.

Immigration officers and procedures

When someone arrives to visit our country, they need to present their travel documents to an Immigration Officer, who checks:

- the visitor's identity – that they look like the same person shown on the passport
- where the person is coming from
- how long they are staying
- the purpose of their stay
- whether they have permission to stay.

Find out about the visa requirements for visiting your country. In pairs, role-play a conversation between a person arriving at an airport or seaport, and an Immigration Officer. Write your dialogue below. It should clearly show what the Immigration Officer's role is.

7 Groups of countries

CARICOM and OECS

1 a Tick (✔) the organisations that each country belongs to as a full member.

b Highlight your country.

Countries	CARICOM	OECS
Anguilla		
Antigua and Barbuda		
The Bahamas		
Barbados		
Belize		
Bermuda		
British Virgin Islands		
Cayman Islands		
Dominica		
Grenada		
Guyana		
Haiti		
Jamaica		
Montserrat		
St. Lucia		
St. Kitts and Nevis		
St. Vincent and the Grenadines		
Suriname		
Trinidad & Tobago		
Turks and Caicos Islands		

2 Find your country on a map of the Caribbean. Write the names of the five islands that are closest to yours and are members of both CARICOM and OECS.

_____
_____
_____
_____

Locating the Caribbean

Understanding our organisations

1. Read the information below and then write the text in the correct column.

CARICOM	OECS

- Aims to promote cooperation and build strength among member states
- Brings together most Caribbean islands, big and small
- Began in 1981
- Formed by the Treaty of Chaguaramas
- Formed by the Treaty of Basseterre
- Brings together small states with one or two main crops
- Has its Head Office in St. Lucia
- Has its Head Office in Guyana
- Began in 1973

2. "The OECS has also integrated the judicial system and currency of member states."

Discuss this statement with a partner. In your words, explain what it means.

HINT

Mention the East Caribbean Central Bank and the Eastern Caribbean Supreme Court.

21

Unit 7 Groups of countries

Welcoming each other

1. Choose another country in the OECS and/or CARICOM which you would like to visit and learn more about.

   a The country or island I would like to visit is _____

   b Reasons I would like to visit: _____

   _____

   c What I would like to learn more about: _____

   _____

2. Compose a short email to a student on your chosen island, inviting them to visit you. Suggest some ideas for what you would like to show them on their visit.

New Message

To

Subject

8 How far?

Drawing a map

Use this page to complete the map drawing activity on page 42 of your textbook. You can use the grid to help you work out the distances between places.

9 Natural features

Sulphur Springs

Read these online reviews about Sulphur Springs in St. Lucia, then answer the questions on the next page.

Sulphur Springs

#5 of 22 things to do in St. Lucia

Overview

Sulphur Springs Park is a world-famous natural feature of the Caribbean. Visitors from all over the world come to enjoy the black water and mud, and learn about the history of the volcano.

🕘 **Opening hours:** Sun–Sat 09:00–17:00

⏱ **Suggested length of visit:** < 1 hour

📍 **Address:** Sulphur Springs Access Road, Soufrière Street, St. Lucia

"We loved the mud baths! Immerse yourself in the four pools at different temperatures, then slather in the volcanic mud. We had such fun."

"Your skin feels amazing after a bath in the healing water. Our guide made the visit interesting with fun facts. Watch out for the smell of sulphur at the volcano!"

"A must do. We did the soak and the mud bath (the best!), and then rinsed under a nearby waterfall. There is a combo deal for the guided volcano tour and the mud bath."

"Wear good walking shoes for the volcano hike, and don't wear your smartest clothes as they will get a bit muddy. A great experience!"

The Caribbean environment

① Which information does the website provide in the listing? (tick (✔) all that apply)

Name of attraction ☐   Opening hours ☐   Visa requirements for the island ☐

Address of the attraction ☐   How long you should spend there ☐

Rating amongst other features on the island ☐

Advice on what to bring and what not to bring ☐

② What extra information do people offer in the reviews?

_____
_____
_____
_____
_____

③ List three activities that people can do at this attraction.

_____
_____
_____

④ Why are the volcano and the hot springs near to each other?

_____
_____
_____

⑤ What did most of the reviewers like most about the attraction?

_____
_____

⑥ Why do you think people like to read other visitors' reviews about an attraction?

_____

⑦ Choose a natural feature you have visited with your family or with your class. Give it a rating out of five stars, and write a short review.

☆☆☆☆☆

Unit 9 Natural features

Volcanoes

Use an atlas. Locate each of the following volcanoes in an atlas, and find their elevation (height above sea level). Use books or the internet to help you find the following information:

- Does its name have a special story?
- Is it active or inactive?
- Does it have a hiking trail or any other attractions?
- Have there been any recent or dangerous eruptions?

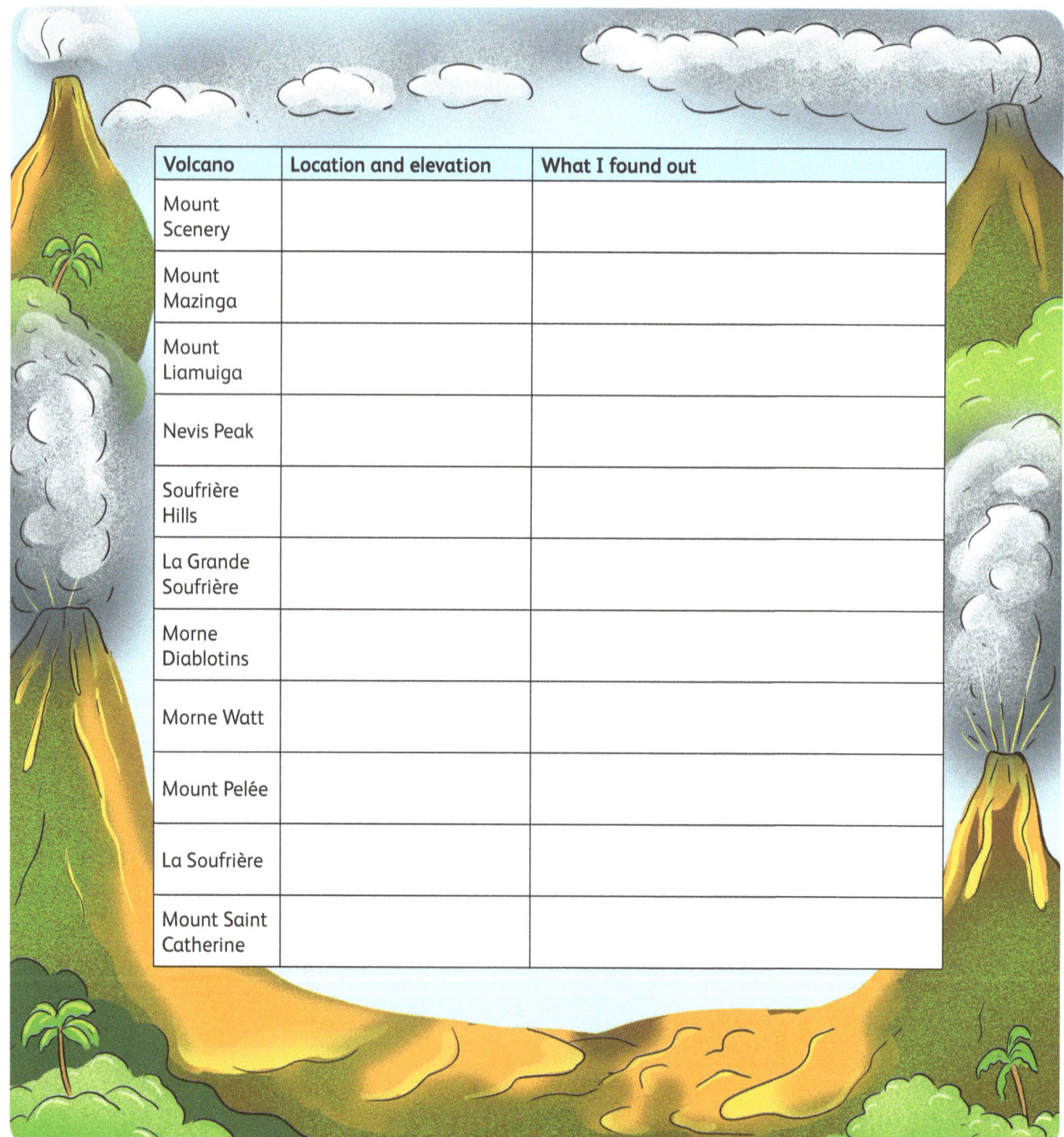

Volcano	Location and elevation	What I found out
Mount Scenery		
Mount Mazinga		
Mount Liamuiga		
Nevis Peak		
Soufrière Hills		
La Grande Soufrière		
Morne Diablotins		
Morne Watt		
Mount Pelée		
La Soufrière		
Mount Saint Catherine		

26

The Caribbean environment

A natural feature near me

Research a natural feature in your area. Write your own fact file about this natural feature and draw or glue a picture of it.

fact file

- Name: ....
- Type of natural feature: ....
- Address: ....
- Activities that people can do here: ....
  ....
  ....
- Opening hours: ....
- Suggested duration of a visit: ....
- Picture:

- Why people like to visit this place:
  ....
  ....

10 Natural disasters

Natural events that cause damage

1. Read each description. Write what kind of natural disaster is being described. Then draw a picture or diagram to illustrate it.

Hot, molten rock from deep underground gets pushed up through a crack in the Earth. Many gases get released into the air. Lava, ash, smoke and rocks can all cause damage when this happens.

This is a very strong storm, with strong winds that move in a swirling, circular direction. In the Caribbean, these usually take place between June and October.

Very heavy rainfall causes huge amounts of water to accumulate, too much to drain away. Many people and animals may drown, and buildings can be badly damaged from the water. Crops and livestock also get destroyed.

This takes place when a place is very hot and dry, and there is not enough rainfall. There is not enough water for crops to grow, and the soil may become too dry and cracked for plants to survive.

This is caused by the movement of tectonic plates, which are large pieces of the Earth's crust. These plates push up against or over one another, causing the Earth's surface to shake. This causes enormous damage to built and natural environments. The severity of these events is measured on the Richter Scale.

The Caribbean environment

2 Have you experienced a natural disaster? Write a poem about what happens in a natural disaster. This can be based on your experience or use your imagination.

Global warming

1 a Read about global warming.

What is global warming?

Global warming is the gradual rise in the Earth's average temperature. This is not the same as the changes that happen from one season to another as part of natural climate patterns. Rather, it is an overall rise in the average temperature on Earth, as well as an overall rise in ocean temperatures.

What causes global warming?

The Earth is warm enough for life to survive because of a natural process called the **greenhouse effect**. This is the effect of gases in the Earth's atmosphere trapping heat from the Sun. However, since the invention of electricity, human activities have started to release huge amounts of **greenhouse gases** into the atmosphere.

These gases include **carbon emissions** and **methane**. These gases cause the **enhanced greenhouse effect**.

In other words, too much heat is trapped in the atmosphere. Human activities that release the most greenhouse gases include:

- burning fossil fuels such as petrol, coal, diesel, gas and oil for power
- cutting down forests for farming, removing trees that help to absorb carbon from the atmosphere
- animal rearing (because cows produce methane gas).

What are the effects of global warming?

Even a 1- or 2-degree rise in the Earth's temperature will cause a huge rise in natural disasters. This includes:

- changes in the world's climate patterns
- more extreme climate events such as hurricanes, earthquakes, droughts and floods
- water shortages in areas that experience hot weather and droughts
- mass extinctions as the oceans heat up and many species of animals and plants are not adapted to live in warmer temperatures
- rising sea levels as the polar caps melt, causing flooding of coastal places and islands.

This has become known as the **climate emergency**.

The Caribbean environment

b Use the information you have read. You can also use books, look at videos or websites on the internet. Write your own headings and captions for these pictures to explain how they illustrate global warming.

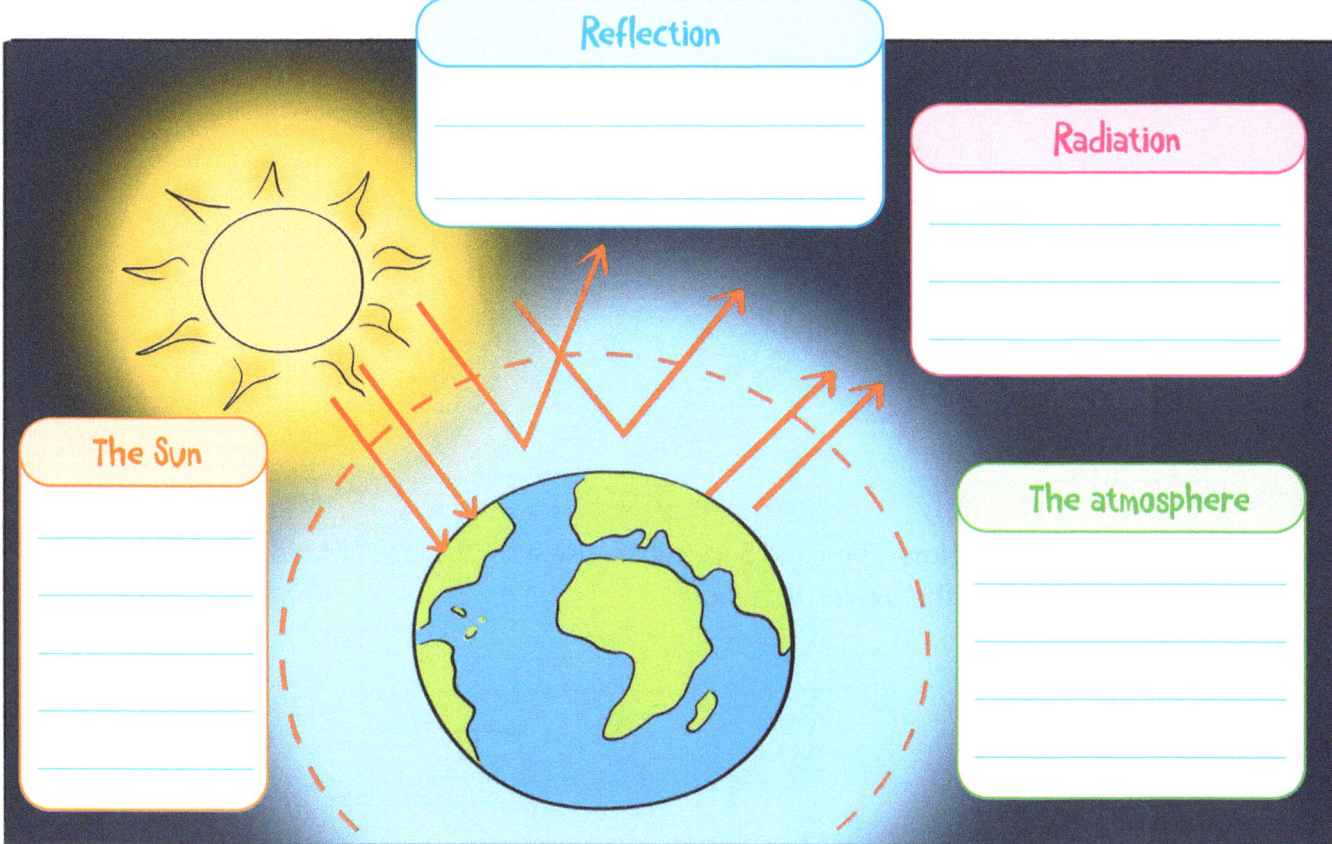

31

Unit 10 Natural disasters

The melting ice caps

1. Label the north and south poles on this globe.

2. Pour 50 ml water into a glass. Then add 5 ice cubes. Use a small piece of tape to mark the water level. Place your glass in the sun for 10 minutes.

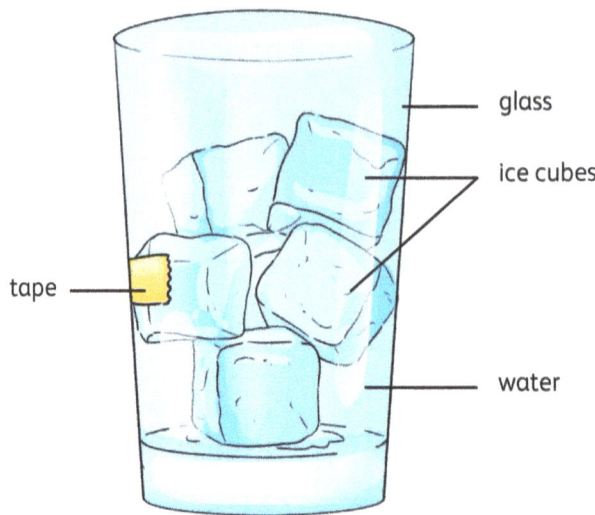

   a   What happens to the water level? _____

   b   What does this tell us about the effects of the melting of the ice caps on Earth?
   _____

3. What would be the effects of a rising sea level for small island nations?

11 Preparing for natural disasters

Being prepared

1 Suggest three ways of keeping well-informed so that you know when a hurricane or volcanic eruption is expected to take place.

_____
_____
_____

2 Imagine that your community has been warned that a Class 3 to 4 hurricane is expected to pass through your area in the next 48 hours. What can you do to make sure you have …

- enough water? _____
- power if the electricity supply is interrupted? _____
_____
- food if the shops are closed for the next few days? _____
_____
- light if there is no power? _____

3 Explain why each of these items of advice are important ways to prepare for a natural disaster.

a   Bring any outside furniture inside.
_____
_____

b   Close or board up windows and glass doors.
_____
_____

c   Make sure your car is filled with petrol and mobile phones are fully charged.
_____
_____

d   Make sure your pets have name tags.
_____
_____

4 Suggest two ways that people can avoid causing wildfire disasters.
_____
_____

Unit 11 Preparing for natural disasters

The Kyoto Protocol and the Paris Agreement

1 Read the information about the Paris Agreement of April 22, 2016.

Every year, the United Nations holds a climate conference called 'Conference of the Parties' or COP for short. COP 21 was held in Paris in 2015. Leaders from 195 countries agreed to work together to reduce the world's carbon emissions over time. The plan included these ideas:

- to keep climate change lower than 1.5 °C
- to achieve 'climate neutrality', in other words a point where global greenhouse gas emissions are no longer increasing
- to increase the sustainability of human life on Earth
- to achieve a balance between the amount of gases entering the atmosphere (for example, by burning non-renewable natural fuels), and the amount being removed (for example, by forests, oceans and the soil, as well as new technologies).

2 Discuss the information you have read, as well as information you can find on the internet or in books. Answer these questions.

a   Name three Caribbean countries that signed the Paris Agreement.

b   Name three non-Caribbean countries that signed the Paris Agreement.

c   Write your own understanding of these terms:

CLIMATE	NON-RENEWABLE NATURAL FUELS

EMISSIONS	SUSTAINABILITY

d   Why is it important for all the world's countries to work together on the issue of climate change? What happens if some countries do not agree?

e   Find out more about your country's policy about reducing carbon emissions. Write what you find out.

12 The human environment

Greening our environment

Tips for greening your environment

- REDUCE REUSE RECYCLE
- PLANT A TREE
- DO NOT LITTER
- FIX DRIPPING TAPS
- TURN OFF THE LIGHTS
- SHOWER INSTEAD OF BATHING
- USE REUSABLE BAGS
- WALK OR RIDE INSTEAD OF DRIVING
- MAKE A COMPOST HEAP
- Add your tip here

1. Write what you understand by 'greening the environment'.

2. Colour the tips in different colours:
   - Use green for the tips that help reduce land and sea pollution.
   - Use blue for the tips that save water.
   - Use yellow for the tips that help reduce carbon emissions.

3. Write three more tips for greening your environment.

4. Find out about your country's environmental programmes. Identify three ways your country is helping to green the environment.

5. Identify two ways your school is helping to green the environment.

13 Why do people work?

Working to meet our needs

1. Brainstorm, then write the different things your family spends money on each month on the mind map. Ask your parents or guardians to help you rank the items (1 being the item most money is spent on).

2. a Why do you think most money is spent on item number 1?
   _____
   _____

   b Which item do you think most money should be spent on? Why?
   _____
   _____
   _____
   _____

3. Write your own definitions.

   key words

   salary ....
   employee ....
   self-employed ....
   unemployed ....
   retired ....
   volunteer ....

14 Jobs in different industries

Different types of jobs

Choose a job you are interested in. Find out more about it. You can:
- find information on the internet
- visit a business where people do this job (you may need to call first and make a request)
- talk to people you know.

Use this questionnaire to help you gather information. You can use the information to report back to your classmates.

Job: ....

Which industry is it in? ....

What do you do in your job? ....

....

....

....

Where do you do your job? ....

....

Do you work alone or with other people? ....

....

What skills do you use each day? ....

....

What are the most interesting parts of the job? ....

....

What makes the job difficult? ....

....

What kind of training or qualifications did you need? ....

....

Any other information? ....

....

....

15 Resources and employment

Natural resources

1. Explain the difference between human resources and natural resources.

   _____
   _____
   _____

2. Water is one of the most important natural resources for life on Earth. Write your ideas about all the ways we use water around the picture.

3. Draw or write the different ways we use natural resources in each category.

Minerals	Agricultural (crops and livestock)	Soil	Water	Fishing

39

What are fossil fuels?

Plants and animals are made of **organic matter**. When the plants and animals died long ago, their remains became trapped in layers of soil and rocks. The softer parts broke down or decomposed. The bones of the animals and more solid plant parts did not decompose and are found today preserved in rocks as solid **fossils**. The decomposed soft parts of the animals and plants became the solid, liquid or gas fossil fuels we use today. They are also known as non-renewable natural energy resources. Read the information about **fossil fuels**. Use it to answer the questions on the next page.

For millions of years, animals and plants have lived and died on Earth.

On land, the dead organic matter broke down into nutrients in the soil. In the sea, organic matter fell to the sea floor.

Over many years, the organic matter got covered with mud and a fine layer of dust called sediment. The layers of mud and sediment built up and trapped the organic matter into thick layers of mud and rock without air.

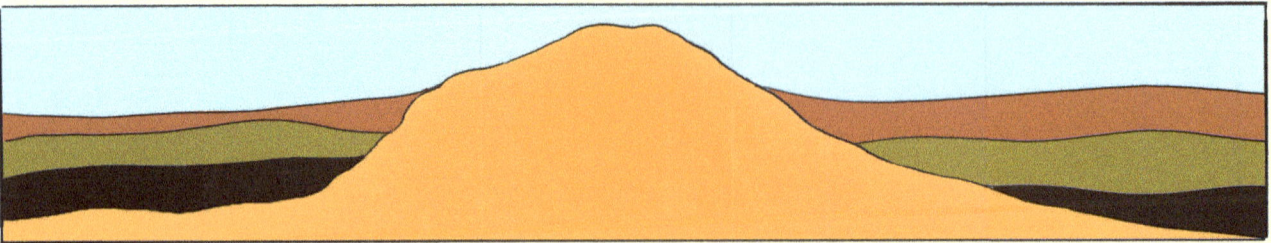

Over thousands of years, more layers of mud and rock formed, with more and more organic matter trapped within. Over time, changes occurred in the Earth's climate. At different times, it got very hot or very cold. This also caused changes in pressure (the force pressing on the rocks). These changes helped turn the organic matter into oil or natural gas.

Work and occupations

This timeline summarises the changes that took place to form fossil fuels.

People have used coal for a long time, but they only began drilling for oil and gas in the 1800s. These resources took around 150 million years to form. However, if humans continue to use them at our current rate, the Earth may only have enough for another 50 years before we run out.

Circle the correct answer.

1. A fossil is …
   a   a kind of soil
   b   prehistoric remains of a plant/animal
   c   oil

2. Fossil fuels formed over …
   a   a few weeks
   b   a few hundred years
   c   millions of years

3. Fossil fuels include …
   a   coal, oil and gas
   b   oil, solar energy and gas
   c   gas, wind power and geothermal energy

4. Fossil fuels formed because …
   a   the Sun's heat cooked the organic matter
   b   the organic matter dissolved in the sea
   c   the organic matter got trapped in layers of rock without air

5. Once we have finished the Earth's supply of oil and gas, will it be possible to produce more? Give reasons for your answer.

   _____
   _____
   _____

6. Countries that signed the Paris Agreement, including some CARICOM countries, have set a target to reduce their use of fossil fuels. Why do you think these countries have done this?

   _____
   _____

Unit 15 Resources and employment

Energy sources

Renewable energy sources are the energy sources that do not easily run out, or that we have continuous access to. Non-renewable energy sources are those that can be used up completely over time.

1 a Match the correct label to each energy source.

b For each picture, write what people use this energy for.

sunshine   wind turbines   volcano   oil rig   gas container

dam with hydroelectric plant

2 Define these terms in your own words:

key words

energy source ....

renewable ....

non-renewable ....

3 Find out which energy sources are used in your country. Tick (✔) those that are widely used.

Gasoline (liquid petroleum) ☐   Hydroelectric power ☐

Petroleum gas (natural gas) ☐   Solar power ☐

Coal ☐   Wind power ☐

42

16 Major Caribbean industries

Tourism

One of the biggest industries in the Caribbean is tourism. Tourists are people who visit a country. There are many kinds of tourism:

* **leisure tourism** – people who visit a country for holidays and fun
* **business tourism** – people who visit for conferences or work reasons
* **medical tourism** – people who visit to get healthcare that they cannot get in their own country, or that they prefer to get in another country.

Caribbean visitors are people who travel from their home country in the Caribbean to other Caribbean countries. Non-Caribbean visitors come from other countries.

1. Visit a tourism office or contact your local tourism authority to do some research about tourism in your country. If possible, find out how many tourists entered the country in:
   a   2018   b   2019   c   2020

2. Why do you think visitor numbers went down in 2020?

3. If possible, find out the following figures for the last calendar year:
   a   How many Caribbean visitors entered the country? _____
   b   How many non-Caribbean visitors entered the country? _____

4. a   Were there more Caribbean or non-Caribbean visitors?

   b   Why do you think this was the case?

Unit 16 Major Caribbean industries

Tourist attractions

A tourist attraction is a place that attracts tourists to visit. It may be a place of natural beauty, such as a beach, a forest or a lookout point. It may be a natural feature such as a volcano, waterfall or mountain path. Some tourist attractions are places of cultural interest such as great houses, museums, churches, cultural centres or local markets. Others involve activities such as snorkeling, scuba diving, hiking or fishing.

List the top four tourist destinations that tourists like to visit in your country. Draw or glue a picture and write a short description.

Work and occupations

The impact of Covid-19

A **pandemic** is an outbreak of disease that affects many people. A **global pandemic** affects countries all over the world. In late 2019, many people began to get sick from Covid-19, a type of virus that can cause breathing problems and other serious complications. Very soon, governments around the world responded with **lockdown restrictions**, such as:

* Airports, seaports and other travel closed to visitors.
* People had to wear masks outside their homes.
* People arriving in a country had to go into quarantine.
* Many international borders were closed to visitors.
* Hotels and resorts had to close.
* Public gatherings were not allowed. Churches, cinemas, theatres and conference centres were all kept closed.
* Schools closed and many students had to be homeschooled or schooled remotely.
* Restaurants and many businesses closed.
* People had to work from home, and many people lost their jobs.

Wash your hands

1. Talk to people in your family.

    a What kinds of restrictions did your family experience?

    _____
    _____
    _____
    _____

    b How did Covid-19 affect your country and your community? Write about it here.

    _____
    _____
    _____
    _____
    _____

17 Trade between Caribbean countries

Understanding regional trade

You have learnt that people work to provide goods and services, so that they can earn money. This is also true of countries.

- Imports are goods and services we buy from other countries. The goods and services come in, via our ports, and money goes out of the country to pay for them.
- Exports are things we sell to other countries. These are goods and services that go out, usually by plane or ship, and money comes into the country to pay for them.

CARICOM has a special council that helps to integrate trade in goods amongst its member countries. This council is called the Council of Trade and Economic Development (COTED).

Look at this map of the Caribbean.

1. Place a red dot on your home country.
2. Place green dots on countries which your home country trades with.
3. Research different products that other countries in the OECS and CARICOM produce. Draw small pictures or labels around the map to illustrate some of the products.

Work and occupations

Our exports and imports

1 Find out which products or services your country exports. Write four of these here.

_____
_____
_____
_____

2 Fill in some other OECS and CARICOM countries in the first column of this table. Then fill in products that your country imports from each country.

Other countries in our region	What my country imports from this country

3 What does COTED stand for? _____

4 What do you think it means to 'integrate trade in goods among its member countries'? What do you think the council does?

_____
_____
_____
_____

5 Explain in your own words the importance of CARICOM.

_____
_____

47

18 National leaders

The Parliament

If possible, go on a visit to the Parliament and learn more about it. You can also find information in books and on the internet.

① Where does the Parliament gather? Write the address and the opening hours. Draw, copy or glue a picture of the building.

② What is the difference between government members and opposition members?
_____
_____

③ Draw a diagram showing the seating arrangements of the Parliament.

④ Describe the functions of the Speaker.
_____
_____
_____
_____

Caribbean nations

Civic responsibility

The leaders we choose for our communities have a responsibility to represent the people that have elected them. This means that citizens have a right to be able to contact their local representative, in order to report matters that affect the community. The ability to reach your local leaders is called **access**. When citizens make use of this right, we can participate in looking after own community.

1. Find out the name and contact details of your area representative.

2. Why is it important to have access to our representatives?

3. Citizens can participate in many different kinds of activities that improve their communities. They may work together to clean the area, improve the facilities available, or build connections and unity in the community. In pairs, brainstorm an idea for an activity that could help or improve your community. Write your idea here.

- Our idea is: ....
....

- Who would be involved: ....
....

- What they would do: ....
....

- How this would improve our community: ....
....
....

19 Belonging to a Caribbean nation

Moral standards

Our moral standards are our beliefs about what is right and what is wrong. Our morals guide our behaviour and our actions. For example, trustworthiness is widely accepted as a good moral standard. This would guide our actions:

Morally unacceptable
- lying
- breaking trust

← Trustworthiness →

Morally acceptable
- speaking the truth
- keeping promises
- honouring commitments

Work with a partner. Brainstorm behaviours that you find morally acceptable and unacceptable, based on these values.

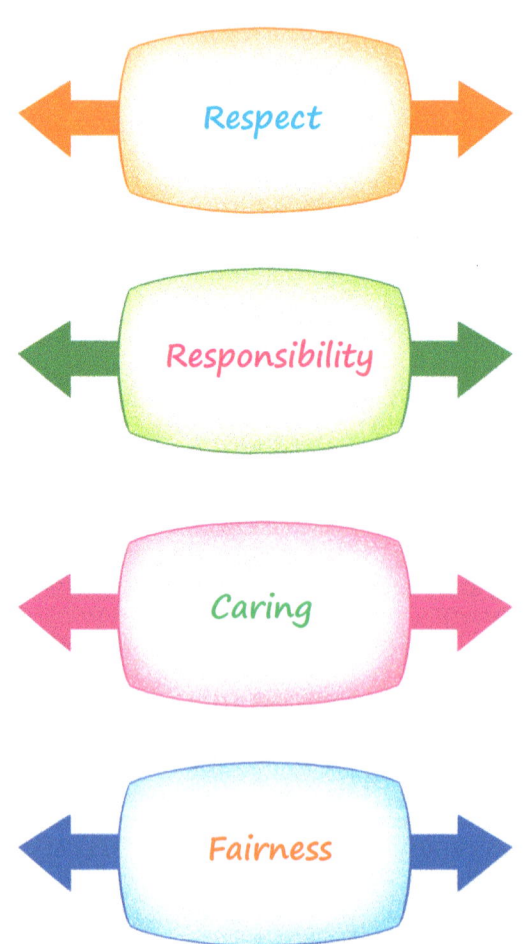

Caribbean nations

Moral behaviour

1 With a partner, brainstorm things you can do at school and in the community that would demonstrate your commitment to the values you explored on page 50.

2 Exemplary conduct means the best possible behaviour. Think of someone at school whose behaviour demonstrates excellent moral standards.

a Describe what kind of behaviour you would describe as exemplary.

b Suggest a way we could recognise exemplary conduct.

c Suggest ways to encourage more children to behave in this way.

_____
_____
_____
_____
_____
_____
_____
_____

3 Some types of behaviour are not wrong morally but may be frowned upon at school. Write three things you can do at home but not at school.

_____
_____
_____

Unit 19 Belonging to a Caribbean nation

Differences of opinion

Sometimes, people may hold differing views about what is morally acceptable and what is morally unacceptable.

1 Read the different statements. Choose one, and write your own views about it.

> My sister is vegetarian. She says it is morally unacceptable to kill animals and eat meat. But I disagree, as long as the animals are kept in humane conditions.

> I know it is unacceptable to lie. But sometimes, telling the truth can hurt people's feelings.

> Sometimes I promise to do something, but then circumstances change and it is not possible to keep my promise. What is the right thing to do?

_____
_____
_____
_____
_____
_____
_____
_____

2 Describe another situation where people might agree on what is morally acceptable.

_____
_____
_____
_____
_____

Caribbean nations

Taking personal and group responsibility

1 As a class, brainstorm the ways that you can take responsibility for moral behaviour as an individual and as a group.

    a Ways I can take responsibility for my own moral behaviour:

    _____
    _____
    _____
    _____

    b Ways that we can take responsibility for our behaviour as a group:

    _____
    _____
    _____
    _____

2 Draw up your own declaration of moral responsibility. Write it here and sign it.

3 What does it mean to have a 'Caribbean identity'? What do people from different countries in the Caribbean have in common? What do we take responsibility for as part of a regional group? Write your own ideas.

_____
_____
_____
_____

Unit 19 Belonging to a Caribbean nation

Resolving conflicts

Sometimes we encounter conflicts, such as disagreements, arguments and fights. Conflict is a normal, natural part of life. We all experience conflict sometimes, with our friends, family members and in our communities. Conflicts also arise between different groups, and between countries. There are different ways to handle conflict:

* **Escalating** the conflict means making it bigger. This is usually unhelpful, but rarely we may choose to escalate a conflict in a controlled way in order to be taken seriously.
* **De-escalating** the conflict means making it less. For example, if you can calm the conflict you will be more likely to understand each other's point of view, which is the first step towards finding a solution.
* **Resolving** a conflict means finding a solution. Both sides need to work together to try to resolve it.

Win–win solutions make all sides feel they have been heard and feel satisfied that their needs are being taken into account. Sometimes we can mediate in a conflict in order to help to resolve it. A mediator is someone who steps in and helps the people involved in the conflict see each other's point of view.

1. Work with a partner. Take turns telling each other about a conflict you have experienced – at home, at school, or anywhere else. Write the main points:
    - Who was involved? _____
    - What happened? _____
    - How did it end? _____
    - How did you feel about it? _____

2. What could have happened to end the conflict differently (either better or worse). Write your thoughts here.
    _____
    _____
    _____

3. Role-play the conflicts you discussed. Use any or some of these techniques to reach a win–win solution. Shade the blocks that your classmates demonstrated in their role plays.

Speak kindly and gently	Think or write about a way to make it better	Talk to each other to work it out	Take turns and share	Find someone else to play with or spend time with
Walk away and take a break	Use 'I' messages I feel … I would like …	Talk to a grown-up or an authority	Count to 10	Have a meeting

20 People are national symbols

My national hero

Choose someone who you see as a hero. It may be one of the figures from your textbook, or someone else you see as a Caribbean national symbol. Find out more about your chosen hero, and complete the fact file.

fact file

- Name: ....
- Date of birth: ....
- Place of birth: ....
  ....
- Personal history: ....
  ....
  ....
  ....
- Achievements: ....
  ....
  ....
  ....
- Why I believe this person is a national hero:
  ....
  ....
  ....

21 National celebrations

A celebration in my country

1. Choose a celebration that you have taken part in. Write about it here. You can draw pictures or glue illustrations or photographs from fliers.

Name of celebration: ....

Time of year/Date: ....

What it celebrates: ....

....

Special costumes or traditional clothing:

Traditional foods we eat:

What we usually do on this day: ....

....

....

Caribbean nations

2 A story about something that I remember about this day:

22 The way we live today

In this unit, you have read about different children and where they live. Write your own story. You can also draw or glue a picture to illustrate your story.

- your name, where you live and who lives with your family

- a description of your family home

- the beliefs and values in your family

- what happens when difficulties arise in your family

- Caribbean traditions that form part of your family life

- ways that your life is similar to, or different from, any of the children you have read about.

Caribbean cultural patterns

23 Cultural links

Arts, culture and sports

1 Complete these mind maps. Write as many different ideas as you can think of.

   a

   b

2 Choose either your favourite sport, or your favourite type of music. Write about it here. Include:
   - the name of the sport or music that you like
   - an event you have attended or heard about
   - which sportspeople or artists you admire
   - when or where you watch or listen to it
   - who in your family or friendship circle enjoys it with you
   - what events you are looking forward to.

24 Sharing our culture using ICT

Sending and receiving messages

1 We communicate in many ways every day. Circle all the kinds of communication you have used this week.

- watching TV
- watching videos online
- sending/receiving emails
- sending a voice note
- reading signs or posters at school
- writing a letter
- sending a text message
- speaking

Hayley is sending a text to her mum. Hayley is the **sender**. What she types into her mobile is the **message**. The text messaging app is the **channel**. Her mum is the **receiver**.

- **SENDER**: The person who sends or starts the communication
- **MESSAGE**: The words, gestures or images that the sender uses
- **CHANNEL**: The medium through which the message moves
- **RECEIVER**: The audience that the sender wants to reach
- **FEEDBACK**: The reply or information that the sender receives back

2 Discuss the model of communication above. Then use different colours to identify and circle the sender, message, channel, receiver and feedback in each situation.

Show your colours in a key. ☐ sender ☐ message ☐ channel ☐ receiver ☐ feedback

a Anna tells her grandmother about an event that happened at school. Her grandmother listens and then asks some questions.

b A radio station broadcasts a daily cooking programme. Some listeners can call in and ask questions.

c Jean-Luke has an online video channel where he posts informative videos. Some of the people who watch can leave comments.

d Claude has a social media account where he sometimes posts pictures and videos. His friends and family can 'like' or comment on his posts.

3 Role-play with a friend to show how a message can be misinterpreted (misunderstood) by the receiver.

Unit 24 Sharing our culture using ICT

Using technology to communicate

In the past, a telephone was a machine that only made telephone calls. You had to dial a number and if the person was home, you could speak to them. Today, our phones have many more functions.

1. a Draw a picture of a mobile phone that you use in your family.
   b Around the mobile phone, list all the different things you use it for.

2. Technology allows us to interact with people that are very far away from us. Think of times you have used a phone or computer to communicate with someone very far away.
   Write an example here.

3. What are the advantages of having a computer at school, and using the internet? Brainstorm with a partner. Write your ideas in the table.

   Advantages of …

… having a computer	… using the internet

   HINT
   Advantages are things that benefit or help us.

Caribbean cultural patterns

Using technology to learn

Have you ever heard the phrase 'There's an app for that'? Today, whatever we are trying to learn or do, there is a program, website, app or video that can help.

Read the information below about some of the apps and software that are commonly used to help with schoolwork. Use a highlighter or marker to underline all those that you have used. Circle those you have not used.

Internet search engines let us put in keywords and search for information. The search engine generates a page of 'hits' – each 'hit' is a link to a website that may offer you more information about your search. If you do an image search, you can look for pictures that relate to your keywords. You can find photographs, illustrations and icons that you can easily copy and print.

You can use **software** such as Word or Google Docs to type up and print out written work. If you need to create tables and graphs, you can use **spreadsheet software** such as Excel or Google Sheets. **Presentation software** such as PowerPoint, Prezi and Google Slides let you create slide presentations on a computer, combining images and text in a digital slide show.

If your computer has mail software such as Mail or Outlook, you might use that for **emails**, but many people get their email online at sites such as Google (Gmail), Yahoo and other mail servers.

YouTube and Vimeo are popular **video sharing** sites. Many people watch videos for news and entertainment, but you can also find videos with instructions and tutorials for any skill you can imagine.

If you are struggling with maths or science, you can find tutorials at free online education sites such as Khan Academy.

During the Covid-19 crisis, many schools had to find ways to teach students who were stuck at home under lockdown. Many schools used apps such as Google Classroom and Zoom to create '**virtual classrooms**'.

63

Unit 24 Sharing our culture using ICT

How we use computers

1. Describe ways that your class has used the computer and the internet to communicate with classes or schools that are far away from you.

   _____
   _____
   _____
   _____
   _____
   _____
   _____

2. Look at the list of apps, programs or websites listed in the box. Circle any that you have used. Put two circles around the ones that you use or like the most. Add the names of any others that you use if they are not already there.

   Choose one of these, and write about:
   - what you use it for
   - why you find it useful
   - what you like about it
   - what you do not like or would change about it.

   | Facebook | Instagram | Twitter | YouTube | GoogleDocs | GoogleMaps |
   | GoogleClassroom | Chrome | Firefox | WhatsApp | Discord | Tiktok |